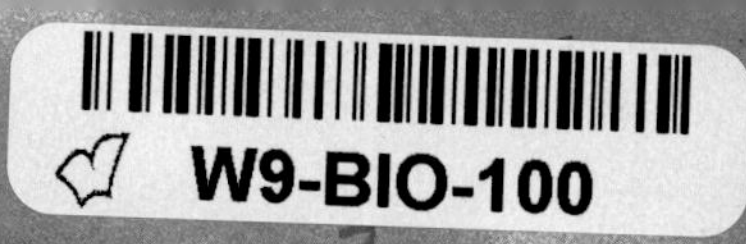
W9-BIO-100

Nuggets of Gold

This is more than an introduction to every book of the Bible;
it is an inspiration.
Here are nuggets of gold from every book of the Bible, with a brief informative introduction to each book of the Bible. God has always been speaking throughout the ages. He is still speaking today.
Here you will hear his voice
which will delight your heart
and feed your soul.

CREATIVE GL PUBLICATIONS

Over the centuries, God has spoken to and inspired ordinary people through the pages of the Bible. In book after book you will hear his voice speaking to you today.

In the wonders of creation, in the struggles of God's chosen people, you will be inspired by the messages recorded by over thirty-five writers, who included a king, a shepherd and a priest.

Sometimes they wrote about hope, while at other times they passed on words of warning. They always wrote a personal message.

Through the pages of this book you will hear God speaking to you.

So

READ

PAUSE

LEARN

as you are inspired by the Book of Books.

Our Wonderful World

In the beginning
God created the heaven and the earth.

God said, Let there be light:
and there was light.

God created man in his own image.

And God saw everything that he made,
and, behold, it was very good.
GENESIS 1:1, 3, 27, 31

Book 1
GENESIS

After the account of God's creation of the world, Genesis relates how Noah built an ark to escape from the great flood. Genesis also tells the story of Abraham, Isaac, Jacob and Joseph.

Rescued!

I will redeem you
with a stretched out arm,
and with great judgments:
and I will take you to me for a people,
and I will be to you a God:
and ye shall know
that I am the Lord your God.
EXODUS 6:6–7

Book 2
EXODUS

Exodus is the book about the ten terrible plagues, and the Israelites' great escape from the land of Egypt, under the gifted leadership of Moses.

Holy, Holy, Holy

I am the Lord
that bringeth you up out of the land of Egypt,
to be your God:
ye shall therefore be holy,
for I am holy.

Sanctify yourselves therefore, and be ye holy:
for I am the Lord your God.
And ye shall keep my statutes, and do them:
I am the Lord which sanctify you.
LEVITICUS 11:45; 20:7–8

Book 3
LEVITICUS

Leviticus takes its title from the priests of the tribe of Levi. This book is about God's holiness. It explains how God's rescued and redeemed people should worship, serve and obey him.

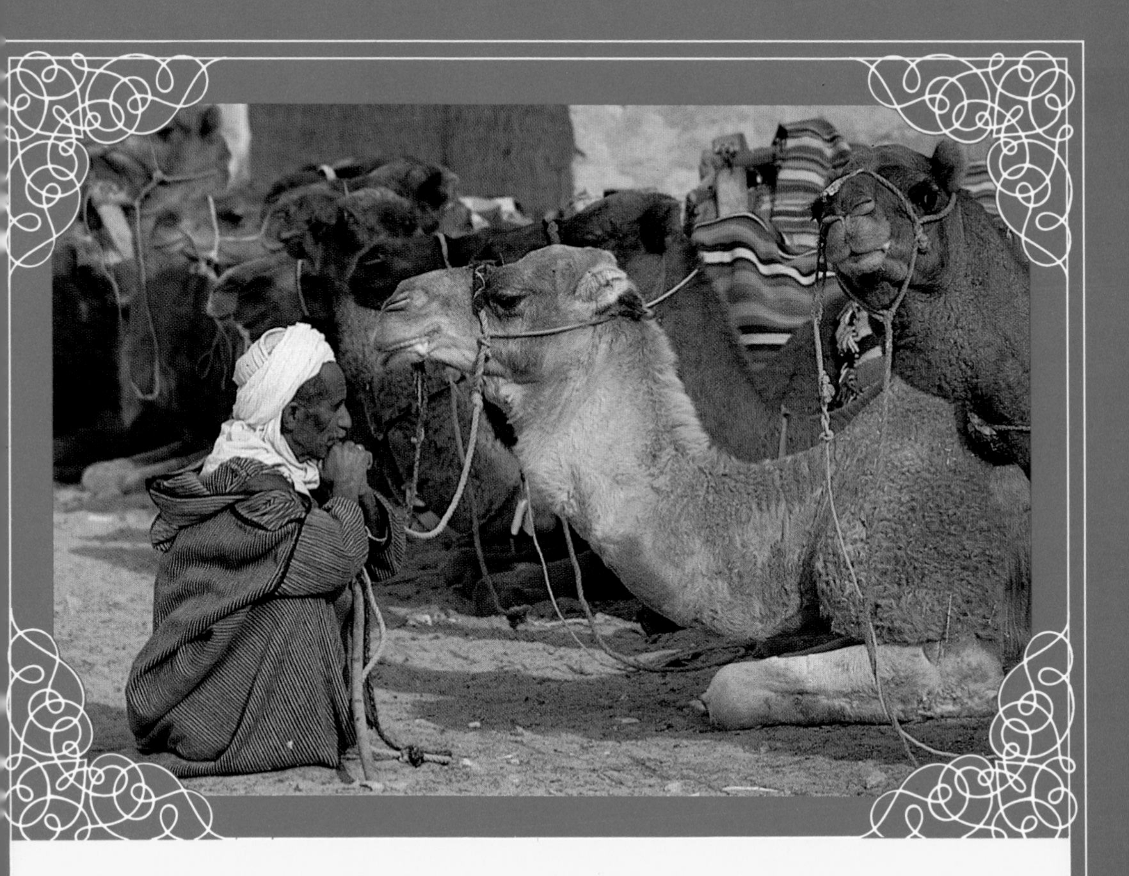

In The Desert

The LORD is longsuffering,
and of great mercy,
forgiving iniquity and transgression …

Pardon, I beseech thee,
the iniquity of this people
according unto the greatness of thy mercy.

The LORD said,
I have pardoned.
NUMBERS 14:18–20

Book 4
NUMBERS

What should have been a two week journey for the Israelites, to arrive in the land God had promised to give them, turned into forty years of wandering around in the desert, and all because of their disobedience to God.

Remember, Remember

And now, Israel,
what doth the Lord thy God require of thee,
but to fear the Lord thy God,
to walk in all his ways,
and to love him,
and to serve the Lord thy God
with all thy heart
and with all thy soul,
To keep the commandments of the Lord.
DEUTERONOMY 10:12–13

Book 5
DEUTERONOMY

As the people of Israel are at last poised to enter the land God had promised to give them, their leader, Moses, counsels them to remember God, and never disobey him, but be blessed by obeying him.

The Promised Land

This book of the law shall not depart out of thy mouth;
but thou shalt meditate therein day and night,
that thou mayest observe to do
according to all that is written therein:
for then thou shalt make thy way prosperous,
and then thou shalt have good success.

So Joshua took the whole land,
according to all that the Lord said unto Moses;
and Joshua gave it for an inheritance unto Israel.
JOSHUA 1:8; 11:23

Book 6
JOSHUA

Joshua becomes the very capable leader of the people of Israel. This book describes the problems they faced during their seven years of conquest, and the settling of the twelve tribes of Israel in the pagan land of Canaan.

Turn Back To God

Because that this people hath transgressed my covenant
which I commanded their fathers,
and have not hearkened unto my voice;
I also will not henceforth drive out
any from before them of the nations
which Joshua left when he died.

In those days there was no king in Israel:
every man did
that which was right in his own eyes.
JUDGES 2:20–21; 21:25

Book 7

JUDGES

The people of Israel ignore and displease God, time and again. Then they turn back to God and are forgiven. Their seventeen judges, who include Gideon and Samson, act as their legal, political and spiritual rulers.

TRUE DEVOTION

And Ruth said,
Intreat me not to leave thee,
or to return from following after thee:
for whither thou goest, I will go;
and where thou lodgest, I will lodge:
thy people shall be my people,
and thy God my God.
RUTH 1:16

Book 8
RUTH

Set in the times of the Judges, here is a touching story about a non-Jewish widow, Ruth. She elects to leave her own country to live with and devote herself to her widowed Jewish mother-in-law, Naomi, in Bethlehem.

THE KINGMAKER

And Samuel said,
Hath the LORD as great delight
in burnt offerings and sacrifices,
as in obeying the voice of the LORD?
Behold, to obey is better than sacrifice,
and to hearken than the fat of rams.
1 SAMUEL 15:22

Books 9 & 10
1 & 2 SAMUEL

Samuel, seen as Israel's last judge and first great prophet, anoints young David to be king elect. Saul is eaten alive with jealousy of David. This portrait of Israel's most famous king shows him warts and all!

THE GREAT SPLIT

If thou wilt walk before me,
as David thy father walked,
in integrity of heart, and in uprightness,
to do according to all that I have commanded thee,
and wilt keep my statutes and my judgments:
Then I will establish
the throne of thy kingdom upon Israel for ever.
1 KINGS 9:4–5

Books 11 & 12
1 & 2 KINGS

Solomon and the building of the Temple in Jerusalem take the centre of the stage in 1 Kings. Then Solomon's divided loyalties towards God are reflected in the break-up of the twelve tribes of Israel into two kingdoms, Israel and Judah.

KING DAVID THE GREAT

Thine, O LORD, is the greatness,
and the power, and the glory,
and the victory, and the majesty:
for all that is in the heaven
and in the earth is thine;
thine is the kingdom, O LORD,
and thou art exalted as head above all.
1 CHRONICLES 29:11

Books 13 & 14
1 & 2 CHRONICLES

1 Chronicles records the spiritual significance of King David's reign, as the writer sets out to encourage the Jews who had returned from exile. 2 Chronicles concentrates on the building and glory of Solomon's Temple.

BACK TO JERUSALEM

Let him go up to Jerusalem, ...
and build the house of the LORD God of Israel.

For Ezra had prepared his heart
to seek the law of the LORD,
and to do it,
and to teach in Israel statutes and judgments.
EZRA 1:3; 7:10

Book 15
EZRA

The book of Ezra records the return of the Jews to Jerusalem after their seventy years of exile in Babylon. The first 50,000 return under Zerubbabel's leadership: 2,000 return with Ezra who rebuilds the spiritual life of the Jews.

REBUILDING FOR GOD

The wall was finished....
And it came to pass,
that when all our enemies heard thereof,
and all the heathen that were about us
saw these things,
they were much cast down in their own eyes:
for they perceived that this work
was wrought of our God.
NEHEMIAH 6:15–16

Book 16
NEHEMIAH

Some thirteen years after Ezra, Nehemiah led the third and last return of the Jews from Babylon to Jerusalem. Under his courageous leadership the shattered walls of Jerusalem were rebuilt, despite all the opposition.

A MOMENT FOR COURAGE

For if thou altogether holdest thy peace at this time,
then shall there enlargement and deliverance
arise to the Jews from another place;
but thou and thy father's house
shall be destroyed:
and who knoweth whether thou art come
to the kingdom for such a time as this?
ESTHER 4:14

Book 17
ESTHER

Esther gives us our only glimpse into the life of the exiled Jews who stayed behind in Persia. Although God's name is not mentioned in the book, his protecting hand is clearly seen in this moving story of Esther's courage.

Suffering Man

Job said,
Naked came I out of my mother's womb,
and naked shall I return thither:
the Lord gave, and the Lord hath taken away;
blessed be the name of the Lord.

For I know that my redeemer liveth.

I know that thou canst do every thing,
and that no thought can be withholden from thee.

JOB 1:21; 19:25; 42:2

Book 18

JOB

Job's four so-called comforters are all wide of the mark with their explanation about why devastating personal tragedy should strike Job. The correct response to suffering is seen in the last chapter of the book when Job worships God.

The Shepherd Song

The LORD is my shepherd;
I shall not want.

He maketh me to lie down in green pastures:
he leadeth me beside the still waters.

He restoreth my soul:
he leadeth me in the paths of righteousness
for his name's sake.

Yea, though I walk
through the valley of the shadow of death,
I will fear no evil:
for thou art with me;
thy rod and thy staff they comfort me.

Thou preparest a table before me
in the presence of mine enemies:
thou anointest my head with oil;
my cup runneth over.

Surely goodness and mercy shall follow me
all the days of my life:
and I will dwell in the house of the LORD
for ever.

PSALM 23

Book 19

PSALMS

The Psalms were Israel's hymn-book; they became the devotional guide for the people of Israel. Above all, they give praise to God for who he is. Here are two of the most famous Psalms.

I HAVE SINNED

Have mercy upon me, O God,
according to thy lovingkindness:
according unto the multitude of thy tender mercies
blot out my transgressions.

Wash me throughly from mine iniquity,
and cleanse me from my sin.

For I acknowledge my transgressions:
and my sin is ever before me.

Against thee, thee only, have I sinned,
and done this evil in thy sight.

Create in me a clean heart, O God;
and renew a right spirit within me.

Cast me not away from thy presence;
and take not thy holy spirit from me.

Restore unto me the joy of thy salvation;
and uphold me with thy free spirit.

PSALM 51:1–4, 10–12

Book 19
PSALMS

Here are two contrasting examples. Psalm 23 illustrates David's trust in the Lord God, even in times of trouble. Psalm 51 is the famous psalm of repentance in which he asks for God's forgiveness and cleansing.

True Wisdom

The fear of the LORD
is the beginning of knowledge:
but fools despise wisdom and instruction.

Trust in the LORD with all thine heart;
and lean not unto thine own understanding.
In all thy ways acknowledge him,
and he shall direct thy paths.

PROVERBS 1:7; 3:5–6

Book 20
PROVERBS

A collection of some 900 inspired, short and pithy proverbs. They give clear moral teaching, and show in very practical ways how to please God.

All Is Vanity

Fear God,
and keep his commandments:
for this is the whole duty of man.
For God shall bring every work into judgment,
with every secret thing,
whether it be good, or whether it be evil.

ECCLESIASTES 12:13–14

Book 21
ECCLESIASTES

Ecclesiastes seeks for the key to the meaning of life. Vanity (mentioned 37 times), the futile emptiness of trying to be happy apart from God, is everywhere. This book shows how life only makes sense as one stands in awe of God.

Love Comes From God

I am my beloved's,
and his desire is toward me.

Many waters cannot quench love,
neither can the floods drown it:
if a man would give all the substance
of his house for love,
it would utterly be contemned.
SONG OF SOLOMON 7:10; 8:7

Book 22
SONG OF SOLOMON

At one level this is a love song written by Solomon. At another level it is a picture of Israel as God's bride, and the church as Jesus Christ's bride.

Salvation

Comfort ye,
comfort ye my people, saith your God.

Surely he hath borne our griefs,
and carried our sorrows:
yet we did esteem him stricken,
smitten of God, and afflicted.
But he was wounded for our transgressions,
he was bruised for our iniquities.

ISAIAH 40:1; 53:4–5

Book 23
ISAIAH

The prophet Isaiah warned Judah not to trust in military alliances but in God's powers. Isaiah taught that salvation, physical and spiritual, only comes from God, not from man.

Come Back To God

Obey my voice,
and I will be your God,
and ye shall be my people.

Behold, the days come, saith the LORD,
that I will make a new covenant
with the house of Israel.

I will put my law in their inward parts,
and write it in their hearts.

JEREMIAH 7:23; 31:31, 33

Book 24
JEREMIAH

For forty years, the prophet Jeremiah called the people of Israel back to God. He had to battle against idolatry, moral decadence and corrupt worship. For his pains, he is imprisoned and beaten and treated as a traitor.

FACING DEVASTATION

It is of the LORD's mercies
that we are not consumed,
because his compassions fail not.
They are new every morning:
great is thy faithfulness.
The LORD is my portion, saith my soul;
therefore will I hope in him.
LAMENTATIONS 3:22–24

Book 25
LAMENTATIONS

Jeremiah cries from the depths of his heart over the destruction of Jerusalem. He confesses Judah's sin, and in the middle of total disaster he recalls how good and faithful God is.

A NEW HEART

A new heart also will I give you,
and a new spirit will I put within you:
and I will take away the stony heart
out of your flesh,
and I will give you an heart of flesh.
And I will put my spirit within you,
and cause you to walk in my statutes.
EZEKIEL 36:26–27

Book 26
EZEKIEL

Ezekiel the prophet keeps alive the hopes of the Jewish exiles in Babylon. This man of visions comforts his people by reminding them that God will one day restore their land to them.

God Rules

Blessed be the name of God for ever and ever:
for wisdom and might are his:
And he changeth the times and the seasons:
he removeth kings, and setteth up kings:
he giveth wisdom unto the wise,
and knowledge to them that know understanding:
He revealeth the deep and secret things.

DANIEL 2:20–22

Book 27

DANIEL

Daniel shows his outstanding faith in God in the lions' den, and rises to become an influential statesman. The story encourages the exiled Jews in Babylon, by emphasising how God rules over the destinities of nations.

I LOVED YOU

*O Israel, return unto the Lord thy God;
for thou hast fallen by thine iniquity.*

*I will heal their backsliding
I will love them freely:
for mine anger is turned away from him.
I will be as the dew unto Israel:
he shall grow as the lily,
and cast forth his roots as Lebanon.*

HOSEA 14:1, 4–5

Book 28
HOSEA

The prophet Hosea's message was given to the northern kingdom of Israel. Hosea's own personal tragedies with his adulterous wife Gomer mirror Israel's spiritual faithlessness to God.

LOCUSTS!

*And it shall come to pass afterward,
that I will pour out my spirit on all flesh;
and your sons and your daughters shall prophesy,
your old men shall dream dreams,
your young men shall see visions.*

JOEL 2:28

Book 29
JOEL

The prophet Joel's message was given to the southern kingdom of Judah. From a recent terrible locust plague, Joel illustrates God's coming day of judgment. Joel urges his hearers to repent before it is too late.

A Bright Future

In that day will I raise up
the tabernacle of David that is fallen,
and close up the breaches thereof;
and I will raise up his ruins,
and I will build it as in the days of old.

Behold, the days come, saith the LORD,
that the plowman shall overtake the reaper,
and the treader of grapes
him that soweth seed;
and the mountains shall drop sweet wine,
and all the hills shall melt.
And I will bring again
the captivity of my people Israel,
and they shall build the waste cities,
and inhabit them;
and they shall plant vineyards,
and drink the wine thereof;
they shall also make gardens,
and eat the fruit of them.

And I will plant them upon their land,
and they shall no more be pulled up
out of their land which I have given them.

AMOS 9:11, 13–15

Book 30
AMOS

To the prosperous northern kingdom of Israel Amos delivers his unpopular message. He speaks against their corrupt business practices and phoney religion. God's judgment is close, but the book ends on a note of hope.

Future Hope

Though thou exalt thyself as the eagle,
and though thou set thy nest among the stars,
thence will I bring thee down,
saith the Lord.

And saviours shall come up on mount Zion
to judge the mount of Esau;
and the kingdom shall be the Lord's.
OBADIAH 4, 21

Book 31
OBADIAH

The Edomites invaded Judah just as Judah was being ransacked by the Babylonians. Obadiah prophesies Edom's downfall and predicts the day when Israel will possess her own land and Edom's as well!

The Reluctant Preacher

But I will sacrifice unto thee
with the voice of thanksgiving;
I will pay that that I have vowed.
Salvation is of the Lord.

I knew that thou art a gracious God,
and merciful, slow to anger,
and of great kindness.
JONAH 2:9; 4:2

Book 32
JONAH

Jonah tries to avoid God's call to preach to the wicked people of Nineveh, but God insists—he sends a storm and a large fish to stop Jonah running away. Jonah learns the lesson that God loves people outside the Jewish race.

WALKING WITH GOD

What doth the LORD require of thee, but to do justly,
and to love mercy,
and to walk humbly with thy God?

Who is a God like unto thee,
that pardoneth iniquity…?

He will subdue our iniquities;
and thou wilt cast all their sins
into the depths of the sea.

MICAH 6:8; 7:18, 19

Book 33
MICAH

Micah is appalled by the oppression of the poor by the rich, and the corrupt judges and religious leaders. He predicts that God will judge the people of Judah for this, but he ends with a message of comfort and hope.

GOD'S JUDGMENT

The LORD is slow to anger,
and great in power.

The mountains quake at him,
and the hills melt.

The LORD is good,
a strong hold in the day of trouble;
and he knoweth them that trust in him.

NAHUM 1:3, 5, 7

Book 34
NAHUM

Nahum the prophet predicts the fall of Nineveh, the arrogant capital city of Assyria. Nineveh's destruction is seen as God's judgment on the Assyrians' neglect of God and on their harshness towards other nations.

A CRY OF FAITH

The just shall live by his faith.

Although the fig tree shall not blossom,
neither shall fruit be in the vines;
the labour of the olive shall fail,
and the fields shall yield no meat;

Yet I will rejoice in the LORD,
I will joy in the God of my salvation.
The LORD God is my strength.

HABAKKUK 2:4; 3:17, 18–19

Book 35

HABAKKUK

'Why do the wicked and cruel Babylonians go unpunished?' asks the prophet Habakkuk. He finds his answer in God's goodness and wisdom, and in the fact that nothing can ultimately thwart God's plans.

The Day of The Lord

The great day of the Lord is near.

Seek ye the Lord, all ye meek of the earth.

The Lord thy God
in the midst of thee is mighty;
he will save,
he will rejoice over thee with joy;
he will rest in his love,
he will joy over thee with singing.
ZEPHANIAH 1:14; 2:3; 3:17

Book 36
ZEPHANIAH

The prophet Zephaniah emphasises the need for the people of Judah to turn away from idolatry, and focuses on their need for personal and spiritual revival. If they repent, God promises to bless them.

Finish The Temple

Thus saith the Lord of hosts;
Consider your ways.
Go up to the mountain,
and bring wood, and finish the house.

And I will shake all nations,
and the desire of all nations shall come:
and I will fill this house with glory,
saith the Lord of hosts.
HAGGAI 1:7–8; 2:7

Book 37
HAGGAI

The Jews are now settled back in Jerusalem, but the rebuilding of the Temple is being neglected. Haggai galvanises them into action as he encourages the people to renew their trust in the Lord.

THE MESSIAH WILL COME

Rejoice greatly, O daughter of Zion;
shout, O daughter of Jerusalem:
behold, thy King cometh unto thee:
he is just, and having salvation;
lowly, and riding upon an ass,
and upon a colt the foal of an ass.
ZECHARIAH 9:9

Book 38
ZECHARIAH

Like Haggai, the prophet Zechariah urges the people of Jerusalem to complete the rebuilding of the Temple. In a series of visions, Zechariah stresses that they must be a holy people. He is certain that the Messiah will come.

RETURN AND REPENT

I have loved you, saith the LORD.

Unto you that fear my name
shall the Sun of Righteousness
arise with healing in his wings;
and ye shall go forth,
and grow up as calves of the stall.
MALACHI 1:2; 4:2

Book 39
MALACHI

The Temple has been rebuilt, and yet the people of Jerusalem still displease God. They worship idols, crush the poor and marry pagans. Malachi urges them to repent and to return to their God, the God of love and justice.

The New Way

From beside the Sea of Galilee, and other places, we have the immortal words of Jesus.

Paul speaks to us in his exciting letters, often dashed off in haste, on one of his many preaching tours.

The big fisherman Peter adds his gentle words of encouragement.

John, the apostle of love, was inspired to write about love, light and life.

GOD'S MESSIAH

Simon Peter answered and said,
Thou art the Christ,
the Son of the living God.

Go ye therefore,
and teach all nations,
and, lo, I am with you alway,
even unto the end of the world. Amen.

MATTHEW 16:16; 28:19–20

Book 40

MATTHEW

Matthew uses numerous Old Testament references to show how Jesus Christ is indeed the long-awaited Messiah. Matthew records a great deal of Jesus' teaching, especially about the kingdom of heaven.

THE SUFFERING SERVANT

And whosoever of you will be the chiefest,
shall be servant of all.
For even the Son of Man
came not to be ministered unto,
but to minister,
and to give his life a ransom for many.

MARK 10:44–45

Book 41

MARK

Mark emphasises that Jesus Christ came as a servant who suffered his death on the cross on behalf of the world. Mark also takes great care to show that Jesus Christ is the Son of God.

Jesus Christ's Compassion

For the Son of man is come
to seek and to save
that which was lost.

Repentance and remission of sins
should be preached in his name
among all nations…
Ye are witnesses of these things.
LUKE 19:10; 24:47–48

Book 42

LUKE

To Dr Luke, Jesus Christ is the Saviour of the world. Luke portrays Jesus Christ's great concern for all people, especially the poor, the ill, the outsiders, the children, the helpless and the rejects of society.

The Son of God

For God so loved the world,
that he gave his only begotten Son,
that whosoever believeth in him
should not perish, but have everlasting life.
For God sent not his Son into the world
to condemn the world;
but that the world through him might be saved.
JOHN 3:16–17

Book 43
JOHN

John sets out to present the life, death, resurrection and teaching of Jesus Christ in such a way that people will come to place their own faith in the Son of God, whose gift to them is eternal life.

The Worldwide Mission

And the word of God increased;
and the number of the disciples
multiplied in Jerusalem greatly;
and a great company of priests
were obedient to the faith.

So mightily grew the word of God
and prevailed.
ACTS 6:7; 19:20

Book 44
ACTS

Dr Luke shows how the first Christians (especially Peter and Paul) lived, and how they spoke about Jesus Christ. Under the direction and power of the Holy Spirit they spread the Christian message as far as Rome.

Peace with God

Therefore being justified by faith,
we have peace with God
through our Lord Jesus Christ:
By whom also we have access
by faith into this grace
wherein we stand,
and rejoice in hope of the glory of God.
ROMANS 5:1–2

Book 45

ROMANS

In a magisterial treatise on the Christian message, Paul shows how God accepts us not because we have been good but because he loves us. All we do is place our grateful trust in Jesus Christ.

Love is The Greatest

Charity suffereth long,
and is kind;
charity envieth not;
charity vaunteth not itself,
is not puffed up.

And now abideth faith, hope, charity, these three;
but the greatest of these is charity.
1 CORINTHIANS 13:4, 13

Book 46
1 CORINTHIANS

The church at Corinth was full of spiritual life. But it also had its fair share of Christians who were behaving in very un-Christian ways. Paul writes to encourage the first and correct the second.

A New Creation

For we preach not ourselves,
but Christ Jesus the Lord;
and ourselves your servants for Jesus' sake.
For God, who commanded
the light to shine out of darkness,
hath shined in our hearts,
to give the light of the knowledge
of the glory of God in the face of Jesus Christ.
2 CORINTHIANS 4:5–6

Book 47
2 CORINTHIANS

False teachers frequently arrived after Paul left! Paul refutes their teachings, and in doing so he relates the tough experiences and persecutions he has faced as a follower of Jesus Christ.

ONLY ONE GOSPEL

I am crucified with Christ:
nevertheless I live;
yet not I,
but Christ liveth in me:
and the life I now live in the flesh
I live by the faith of the Son of God,
who loved me,
and gave himself for me.
GALATIANS 2:20

Book 48
GALATIANS

Paul taught that the only way to God is through trust in Jesus Christ. Paul reserves some of his most blunt words for those Galatian Christians who were being wooed away from this basic Christian teaching.

Spiritual Blessings

Even when we were dead in sins,
he hath quickened us together with Christ,
(by grace ye are saved;)...

For by grace
you have been saved through faith;
and that not of yourselves:
it is the gift of God.
EPHESIANS 2:5, 8

Book 49
EPHESIANS

Paul rehearses the wonderful spiritual privileges which God has made available to all Christians—forgiveness, God's acceptance of us, grace, the sealing of the Holy Spirit, etc.—before he says, 'Be united to one another.'

Rejoice in The Lord

Rejoice in the Lord alway:
and again I say, Rejoice.

And the peace of God,
which passeth all understanding,
shall keep your hearts and minds
through Christ Jesus.
PHILIPPIANS 4:4, 7

Book 50
PHILIPPIANS

Paul, under the shadow of the death sentence, writes from his prison cell, and encourages the Philippian Christians to take heart and rejoice in the Lord, as they face persecution and false teachers.

CHRIST IS SUPREME

If ye then be risen with Christ,
seek those things which are above,
where Christ sitteth on the right hand of God.
Set your affection on things above,
not on things on the earth.

And whatsoever ye do, do it heartily,
as to the Lord, and not unto men.
COLOSSIANS 3:1–2, 23

Book 51
COLOSSIANS

When Paul heard that some Christians at Colossae were polluting and diluting Christian teaching with dangerous false teaching, he dashed off this letter, to emphasise that Christ alone is supreme in everything.

CHRIST WILL RETURN

And the Lord make you to increase
and abound in love one toward another,
and toward all men,
even as we do toward you:
To the end
he may stablish your hearts unblameable
in holiness before God.
1 THESSALONIANS 3:12–13

Books 52 & 53
1 & 2 THESSALONIANS

As a result of Paul's preaching at Thessalonica some people became followers of Christ and they remained dear in Paul's heart. He writes to encourage them in their new found faith, and to answer their questions about Christ's return.

MY DEAR SON ...

Follow after righteousness, godliness,
faith, love, patience, meekness.
Fight the good fight of faith,
lay hold on eternal life,
whereunto thou art also called,
and hast professed a good profession
before many witnesses.
1 TIMOTHY 6:11–12

Books 54 & 55
1 & 2 TIMOTHY

The ageing Paul writes to encourage his young protégé Timothy. Paul touches on false teaching, how to run a church, how to worship in church and the kind of people church leaders should be. 2 Timothy is Paul's last letter.

Live for God

The kindness and love of God
our Saviour toward man appeared,
Not by works of righteousness
which we have done,
but according to his mercy he saved us,
by the washing of regeneration,
and renewing of the Holy Ghost.
TITUS 3:4–5

Book 56
TITUS

Paul writes to advise the young minister Titus, who is helping the new Christian church on the island of Crete. He advises about the appointment of church leaders and how all church members must live lives pleasing to God.

Your Runaway Slave

Receive him for ever;
Not now as a servant,
but above a servant,
a brother beloved, specially to me,
but how much more unto thee,
both in the flesh and in the Lord?
PHILEMON 15–16

Book 57
PHILEMON

This is the only private letter of Paul to survive. He urges his good friend Philemon to receive back his runaway slave Onesimus, since he has now become a follower of Jesus Christ.

Jesus Christ is The Best

Wherefore seeing we also are compassed about
with so great a cloud of witnesses,
let us lay aside every weight,
and the sin which doth so easily beset us,
and let us run with patience
the race that is set before us.
HEBREWS 12:1

Book 58
HEBREWS

The unknown author of this letter emphasises that Jesus Christ is far superior to the Old Testament prophets and priests. To strengthen the faith of some wavering Jewish Christians Jesus Christ is presented as the only Saviour.

FAITH AND WORKS

But be ye doers of the word,
and not hearers only,
deceiving your own selves.

Faith, if it hath not works,
is dead, being alone.

Blessed is the man
that endureth temptation.
JAMES 1:22; 2:17; 1:12

Book 59
JAMES

James challenges his readers to live out a true Christian faith and so bring honour and credit to Christ. He emphasises that Christians should both have faith in God and be engaged in doing good deeds.

FAITH UNDER ATTACK

Beloved, think it not strange
concerning the fiery trial
which is to try you,
as though some strange thing happened unto you:
But rejoice,
inasmuch as ye are partakers of Christ's sufferings;
that, when his glory shall be revealed,
ye may be glad also with exceeding joy.
1 PETER 4:12–13

Books 60 & 61
1 & 2 PETER

The storm clouds of persecution are gathering. Peter, the rugged fisherman, pens 1 Peter in order to strengthen the Christian faith of those about to walk through the fires of persecution. In 2 Peter the false teachers are countered.

GOD IS LOVE

These things have I written unto you
that believe on the name of the Son of God;
that ye may know that ye have eternal life,
and that ye may believe
on the name of the Son of God.

Hereby perceive we the love of God,
because he laid down his life for us.
1 JOHN 5:13; 3:16

Books 62, 63 & 64

1, 2 & 3 JOHN

1 John tells people who had become followers of Jesus Christ how to be sure about their Christian faith. The readers of 2 John are told to hang on to true Christian teaching while 3 John encourages hospitality for travelling Christians.

Fight For The Faith

Now unto him
that is able to keep you from falling,
and to present you faultless
before the presence of his glory
with exceeding joy.
To the only wise God our Saviour,
be glory and majesty, dominion and power,
both now and ever. Amen.
JUDE 24–25

Book 65
JUDE

How do you stop followers of Christ from being led astray by false teachers? Jude says, 'become strong in your Christian faith and then you will not be lured away.'

The Book of Visions

Behold, I stand at the door, and knock:
if any man hear my voice,
and open the door,
I will come in to him,
and will sup with him, and he with me.

The Lord God giveth them light:
and they shall reign for ever and ever.
REVELATION 3:20; 22:5

Book 66
REVELATION

With the persecution, imprisonment and killing of Christians being the order of the day, John, exiled on Patmos, writes to inspire Christians to be strong in their faith. His message is that God is still in control.